THE PURSUIT

OF

JESUS CHRIST SERIES

Navigating the Christian Journey with Assurance, Comfort, and Victory

LAYING ON OF HANDS

Edward Karanja

Copyright

THE PURSUIT OF JESUS CHRIST SERIES
LAYING ON OF HANDS

For permission, contact the author:
Reverend/ Chaplain Edward Karanja
Destiny of Christians Intl. Ministries
4143 Green Field Drive
Douglasville, GA 30135, USA
Phone:4048957774/4709891163.
Email: docministries2019@gmail.com
Website: http://www.destinyofchristians.org

ISBN: 9798342602952

Acknowledgments

The support of my spouse, Pastor Tabitha, with her spirit-led input; our daughter Faith and her spouse Jonathan, with their young daughter River, as well as my son Moken and his spouse Tamika; my son Baraka and his spouse Lucy were invaluable to me. Their commitment to ensuring the successful publication of the message contained in this book has not been in vain, for in due season they shall reap abundantly.

Dedication

The entire publication of the message contained in this book is dedicated to the Holy Spirit, who initiated the message and subsequently instructed that it be written down for many to read it and be blessed thereby.

Contents

OPENING PRAYER

Heavenly Father,

We humbly come before You with grateful hearts, seeking Your presence as we embark on this journey of understanding the ministry of laying on of hands and its role in our walk with Christ. Lord, we thank You for the power of Your Spirit that moves through Your people, for the blessings You release, and for the grace You impart through this sacred act.

Holy Spirit, illuminate our understanding and deepen our faith. May each reader be encouraged, edified, and equipped to carry out Your will. As we open this book, we ask for wisdom and revelation. Let every page guide us deeper into Your truth and stir in us a greater awareness of how You use us as vessels to touch the lives of others. May we grow in faith, trust, and obedience, learning to walk in the fullness of Your purpose for our lives.

Lord, we desire to grow in spiritual maturity, moving beyond the elementary teachings and stepping into the deeper truths of our Christian journey, including the powerful practice of laying on of hands. Bless every reader, Lord. May their hearts be open, their spirits be stirred, and their lives transformed by the truths they discover within these pages. We ask this in the mighty name of Jesus, our Savior and Redeemer. Amen.

Introduction

"Therefore, leaving the discussion of the elementary principles of Christ, let us go on to perfection, not laying down again the foundation of repentance from dead works and of faith toward God, of the doctrine of baptisms, of laying on of hands, of the resurrection of the dead, and of eternal judgment." Hebrews 6:1-2

The book of Hebrews 6:1-2 lists six basic truths that constitute the journey of a Christian towards spiritual maturity. It is impossible to mature without the knowledge of these six basic truths. The starting point of a Christian's journey must start with **repentance from dead works**. Repentance is then logically followed by **faith toward God**. The third basic truth is **baptisms**, which refers to both water baptism and baptism in the Holy Spirit. These first three basic truths are explored in the first two books in the series, The Pursuit of Jesus Christ, by this author.

The fourth basic truth, the ministry of **laying on of hands**, is the subject of discussion for this book, which looks at the biblical origin of this ministry in the Old Testament, the biblical evidence of its operation in the New Testament, the purposes of laying on of hands, and the good and potentially bad that should be considered about this ministry.

The above verse calls these teachings of Christ "elementary" or basic because they are the foundation blocks of a firm and solid Christian journey. Just like the others, the ministry of laying on of hands is a foundational block without which the Christian journey to maturity will be incomplete. That is why it is important to know what this ministry is all about.

I call upon the Holy Spirit, the author of the Christian Bible's holy scriptures, to guide and grant us an understanding of the scriptural truth of the ministry of laying on of hands as we progress in our Christian journey toward maturity.

Chapter 1

LAYING ON OF HANDS IN THE OLD TESTAMENT

"And Israel stretched out his right hand, and laid it upon Ephraim's head, who was the younger, and his left hand upon Manasseh's head, guiding his hands wittingly; for Manasseh was the firstborn. And he blessed Joseph, and said, God, before whom my fathers Abraham and Isaac did walk, the God which fed me all my life long unto this day," Genesis 48:14-15

The ministry of laying on of hands is an essential foundational block that every Christian needs in their Christian journey. This ministry is widely used today in churches and is well-accepted and, in most cases, expected by many believers. This section looks at the biblical basis of the ministry of laying on of hands.

First, we will look into the Old Testament to examine scriptures concerning the laying on of hands. The first scripture we find is Genesis 48:12-19:

"So, Joseph brought them from between his knees, and he bowed down with his face to the earth. And Joseph took them both, Ephraim with his right hand toward Israel's left hand, and Manasseh with his left hand toward Israel's right hand, and brought them near him. Then Israel stretched out his right hand and laid it on Ephrim's head, who was the younger, and his left hand on Manasseh's head, guiding his hands knowingly, for Manasseh was the firstborn. Now, when Joseph saw that his father laid his right hand on the head of Ephraim, it displeased him, so he took hold of his father's hand to remove it from Ephraim's head to Manasseh's head. And Joseph said to his father, "Not so, my father, for this one is the firstborn; put your right hand on his head." But his father refused and said, "I know, my son, I know. He also shall become a people, and he also shall be great, but truly his younger brother shall be greater than he, and his descendants shall become a multitude of nations."

In these verses, we are introduced to Jacob, who is also called Israel, laying his hands on Joseph's two sons, Ephraim and Manasseh. Genesis 48:14 says, "Then Israel stretched out his right hand and laid it on Ephraim's head who was the younger, and his left hand on Manasseh's head, guiding his hands knowingly, for Manasseh was the firstborn." Being the firstborn, Manasseh was traditionally expected to receive the greater blessing by Jacob laying his right hand on him. However, guided by the Spirit of God, Jacob deliberately laid his left hand on Manasseh and, instead, laid his right hand on Ephraim, who was younger. The right hand carried heavier blessings than the left hand. Joseph tried to correct his father by actually holding his father's right hand and moving it to Manasseh, saying to his father in Genesis 48:18, "Not so my father, for this one is the firstborn; put your right hand on his head." In the following verse 19, it reads, "but his father refused, and said, 'I know, my son, I know.'" Jacob proceeded to declare greater blessings on the younger child, Ephraim. We will discuss this further in a later chapter.

The next scripture is found in Numbers 27:18. Moses is specifically commanded to lay his hands on Joshua. God did not permit Moses to enter the promised land because earlier, he disobeyed God's instructions to speak to the rock to give water and instead hit it. God told him he would not enter into the Promised Land. Moses then asked the Lord to appoint another leader to lead the people into the Promised Land, and this was God's answer to Moses in Numbers 27:18, which says, "And the Lord said to Moses: 'Take Joshua the son of Nun with you, a man in whom is the Spirit and lay your hand on him.'" Later on, we read in Deuteronomy 34:9, "Now Joshua the son of Nun was full of the spirit of wisdom, for Moses had laid his hands on him."

Next, when we examine Leviticus 1:4, we see that God required his people to lay their hands on the head of their burnt animal sacrifice for the atonement of their sins to be accepted, instructing, "Then he shall put his hand on the head of the burnt offering, and it will be accepted on his behalf to make atonement for him."

Finally, we come to another scripture describing the laying on of hands in Leviticus 16: 20-21. This scripture describes the sacrifices required on the day of atonement, during which the High Priest would enter into the Holy of Holies. God permitted the High Priest to enter into the Holy of Holies only once a year, but first, the High Priest was required to offer a bull as a sin offering for himself and his family. He had to sprinkle some of the bull's blood with his finger onto the mercy seat, which was in the Holy of Holies, seven times. The mercy seat is the cover or lid of the Ark of the Covenant.

He was then instructed to take two goats; one goat was to be killed as a sin offering for the people. God then gave specific instructions about the second goat. First, the High Priest had to cast lots for the two goats: one for the Lord and the other for the goat described as the "scapegoat."

The goat for the Lord was the one to be killed, and some of its blood was brought into the Holy of Holies and sprinkled on the mercy seat seven times. Instructions about the scapegoat are found in Leviticus 16:21, saying, "Aaron shall lay both his hands on the head of the live goat, confess over it all the iniquities of the children of Israel, and all their transgressions, concerning all their sins, putting them on the head of the goat, and shall send it away into the wilderness by the hand of a suitable man." It must be emphasized here that the instructions to Aaron, the High Priest, to lay hands on the scapegoat were given by God Himself. In the New Testament, we come to learn that Jesus Christ is our scapegoat because the sin of the world was laid on him. The instructions about the scapegoat in Leviticus 16:21 foreshadow Christ Jesus, who became our scapegoat by taking our sins away! John, the Baptist, when he saw Jesus coming towards him, said, "Behold the Lamb of God who takes away the sin of the world!" Every person who would lay their hands of faith on Jesus by believing in Him has their sins transferred to Jesus by a supernatural act of God the Father. Just like the scapegoat in Leviticus 16 was led into the wilderness bearing the sins of the people of Israel, so was Jesus led to the cross bearing the sins of the world and, consequently, the sins of every human being.

From the above scriptures, it is clear that the ministry of laying on of hands is well established in the Old Testament. When one looks at the Old Testament, there are specific purposes for the laying on of hands: to transmit blessings, to transmit wisdom, to commission leaders, and to transfer sins.

Now that we have looked at the ministry of laying on of hands in the Old Testament, we will turn our attention to the New Testament.

Chapter 2

LAYING ON OF HANDS IN THE NEW TESTAMENT

And these signs shall follow them that believe; In my name shall they cast out devils; they shall speak with new tongues; They shall take up serpents; and if they drink any deadly thing, it shall not hurt them; they shall lay hands on the sick, and they shall recover. Mark 16:17-18

In the previous section, attention was given to the ministry of laying on of hands in the Old Testament. In this section, attention will be given to the ministry of laying on of hands as found in the New Testament. We will again look at scriptures that talk specifically about this ministry.

Our first reference, Mark 16:17-18 reads, "In my name, they will lay hands on the sick." Our Lord Jesus Christ spoke this as He gave the disciples and all believers the great commission. He specifically mentioned the ministry of laying on of hands for the purpose of physical healing. Today, this particular ministry is regularly practiced in many churches.

The second scripture I want to highlight is 1 Timothy 5:22, in which Paul instructs Timothy, "Do not lay hands on anyone hastily, nor share in other people's sins; keep yourself pure." This is another scriptural confirmation of the practice of laying on of hands in the New Testament.

The third scripture to support the laying on of hands is Mark 10:16, which tells us, “And He took them up in his arms, laid his hands on them, and blessed them." This scripture refers to the time children were brought to Jesus Christ, but the disciples rebuked the parents. The scripture says Jesus was displeased by the disciple's actions and welcomed the children, laying hands on them and releasing a blessing on them.

Another instance of this ministry in operation in Luke 4:40, which tells us, "When the sun was setting, all those who had any that were sick with various diseases brought them to Him, and He laid His hands on every one of them and healed them." It is clear then that the ministry of laying on of hands should not be taken lightly, as our Lord and Savior Jesus Christ exercised it and included it in the Great Commission.

Even more evidence can be found in the New Testament confirming that the ministry of laying on of hands was a common practice. In Acts 8:17, Peter and John laid hands on the Samaritan believers after being evangelized by Phillip, and they received the Holy Spirit; in Acts 6:6, the apostles laid hands on the seven men selected to serve tables, among them, Stephen and Phillip to commission them for this task for which they were selected.

Finally, there is one more scripture of great interest found in James 5:14-15. This scripture is addressed to those believers who are sick, stating, "Let him call for the elders of the church, and let them pray over him, anointing him with oil in the name of the Lord."

Anointing people is always instinctively accompanied by the laying on of hands, as is witnessed in every case today when believers are anointed. The minister would anoint first and then lay hands while praying over the person being anointed. However, it is biblical to lay hands without anointing and acceptable to anoint without laying on hands. There are occasions when oil is poured on someone without touching that person. In Exodus 29:7, God instructed Moses to anoint Aaron in this manner, saying, "Then you shall take the anointing oil, and pour it on his head and anoint him."

Many times, we find that many ministers of the gospel combine anointing with oil, as James 5:14-15 instructs, with laying on of hands. It must, however, be understood that anointing is reserved for church members or those already saved. It is important to note that the scripture is addressed to those who are already members of a church, emphasizing the need to belong to a church.

In concluding this section, it must also be emphasized that the ministry of laying on of hands, as well as anointing, is based on faith in the name of our Lord and Savior, Jesus Christ. He is the Healer. The Minister performing the laying on of hands and anointing, as well as the person being laid hands on and anointed, must both put their faith that the Lord will respond. The oil symbolizes the healing power of the Holy Spirit; the oil itself has no ingredients for healing. Anointing, as some people believe, is not in preparation for death, but rather, it is to impart divine life into the body of the sick person.

One important question lies in James 5:14 that needs to be answered: "Is anyone sick? Call for the elders." The question is, whom should a sick believer call first, the church elders or the doctor? This question will be addressed in the next section.

Chapter 3

CALL THE ELDERS OF THE CHURCH

"Is anyone among you sick? Let him call for the elders of the church, and let them pray over him, anointing him with oil in the name of the Lord. And the prayer of faith will save the sick, and the Lord will raise him up. If he has committed sins, he will be forgiven." James 5:14

Whom should a sick believer call first, the church elders or the doctor? The laying on of hands goes hand in hand with anointing, as indicated in James 5:14, where a sick person is instructed to call the church elders, who would then pray over him, "anointing him with oil in the name of the Lord." This raises a very important consideration for believers: whom do you call first when you get sick? The doctor or the church elders? Consider again this scripture in James 5:14: "Is anyone among you sick? Let him call for the elders of the church."

Almost always, this instruction is hardly considered by believers as a first alternative to calling a doctor or rushing to the hospital. Some would consider calling a doctor first as evidence of a lack of faith in the Lord, the healer, but is it? What about an emergency when every minute counts?

To seek a satisfactory answer to this issue, we must find out the biblical view on doctors, physicians, and medicine. To start, let's examine 2 Kings 1:1-4. King Ahaziah of Samaria, the capital of the Northern kingdom of Israel, was injured after falling through the lattice of his upper room. So, he sent messengers to the idol god Baal-Zebub at Ekron to inquire whether or not he would recover instead of inquiring from the Living God. Elijah, the prophet, instructed by the Lord, intercepted the messengers with a message to King

Ahaziah in 2 Kings 1:3 stating, "Is it because there is no God in Israel that you are going to inquire of Baal-Zebub, the idol in Ekron?" Elijah ended the message by saying that the king would not recover but would die. In this incident, God was completely against seeking answers about health from idols. In this case, the king would have been well advised to seek the Living God first for his healing. Obviously, he had no faith in the Lord the Healer. This case illustrates that God is completely against the idea of seeking healing from supernatural powers of darkness.

Another reference is found in 2 Chronicles 16:12-13. In this case, Asa, the king of Judah, became severely diseased in his feet: "yet in his disease, he did not seek the Lord, but the physicians," and ended up dying soon after he got sick. This is an interesting scripture because it informs the reader that there were physicians available to treat people. The mistake King Asa made was that he deliberately avoided asking the Lord for his healing. It should be noted that God was not against the physicians but against the king's deliberate decision not to seek the Lord first: he despised God's ability to heal him and opted for a physician.

A third reference is in Revelation 3:18; the lukewarm church of Laodicea was instructed to "Anoint your eyes with eye salve, that you may see." Laodicea was famous for producing powdered medicine from Phrygian rock used to treat eye ailments. The Lord referred to it to teach the Laodiceans that they needed to seek the Lord to receive spiritual sight and see their spiritual nakedness. The point, however, is that this eye medicine was widely used to treat eye troubles. The Lord was not condemning the use of eye salve, but rather, He was referring to spiritual sight that can only come from Him.

A fourth reference is found in Luke 10:33-34. This is the story of the good Samaritan who treated a man beaten by thieves. As Jesus told this story, He said the good Samaritan treated the man's wounds with oil, wine, and bandages. This scripture points out the use of oil and wine as some form of medication.

A fifth reference is Luke 5:31. Jesus spoke in this manner: "Those who are well, have no need of a physician, but those who are sick." This scripture points out the necessity of physicians in the medical field. They exist for the sick to go to for medication.

Finally, an interesting case is found in Isaiah 38:21. King Hezekiah was sick, and the prophet Isaiah was sent to tell him he would die. Hezekiah pleaded with the Lord and was granted 15 more years to live. Isaiah then instructed his servants to place a lump of fig tree leaves on Hezekiah's boil. Examining these scriptures, it is clear that scripture is not against physicians or medicine.

The following observations can consequently be made concerning the issue raised by James 5:14 about calling the elders when a believer falls sick:

- First, calling the elders is an open invitation to sick believers.
- Second, elders can be called irrespective of whether a believer is at home or in the hospital, whether or not a doctor is already in attendance, whether one is under medication, and whether or not one has called an ambulance. Many believers call for their

pastors while in hospital. It must be remembered that physicians are a gift in the medical profession to attend to the health of the sick.

- Third, the Lord is the healer irrespective of the presence of a doctor, whether one is in a hospital or at home, and regardless of whether or not one is under medication.
- Fourth, calling elders when you have a doctor or are in hospital is an expression of faith in the Ultimate Healer, the Lord Jesus; otherwise, why call the elders if a doctor is already attending to you or one is already in hospital?
- Fifth, the guiding principle in each situation is given in Proverbs 3:5- 6, which says, "He shall direct your path." There is a similar instruction in Psalm 32:8, "I will teach you and

instruct you in the way you should go. I will guide you with My eye."

Chapter 4

THE PURPOSES OF THE MINISTRY OF LAYING ON OF HANDS

"At sunset, the people brought to Jesus all who had various kinds of sickness, and laying his hands on each one, he healed them." **Luke 4:40**

Scripture reveals that there are at least five purposes mentioned in the scriptures for the laying on of hands. They are 1) Healing, 2) Impartation of the Holy Spirit and Gifts, 3) Commissioning for Ministry, 4) Blessing, and 5) Consecration. Each purpose will be introduced and discussed subsequently.

Transmission of healing is the first purpose that we will discuss along with the process of healing. The Word of God says in Mark 16:18, "...they shall lay hands on the sick, and they shall recover." God is not limited to a particular healing method but heals in diverse ways. In the ministry of laying on of hands, a transfer of God's supernatural power of healing takes place. The healing is entirely the Holy Spirit's work, and the person laying on hands is only an instrument through which God works by his Holy Spirit. The Holy Spirit in scripture is called the Spirit of life (Romans 8:2). Consequently, He imparts life of healing to the sick person. Romans 8:11 tells us, "He who raised Christ from the dead will also give life to your mortal bodies through His Spirit who dwells in you." The reference to "mortal bodies" points to the living physical body of a person. Obviously, the person who is laying hands on a sick person must have faith in divine healing.

The process of healing can be instant or gradual. When healing is instant, the person healed would, in most cases, feel the power of God going through his body. At times, however, healing may not be instant; it may be experienced over time. Many believers can testify to this.

Healing can also be partial or incomplete. This may occur when a person ceases to believe in the healing and gives up, especially when it is gradual healing over time. People who are not healed instantly through the laying on of hands have a challenging time as they try to comprehend why they are not healed instantly when they are prayed for and hands have been laid on them. One question that arises in their minds is about their faith. They begin to wonder whether or not they have enough faith. The issue is complicated when it is suggested that they did not get healed in the first place because they do not have enough faith. Such a remark is devastating to them when they know they desperately need healing. In order to encourage such people, we need to look at specific scriptures related to this problem.

The first case is that of the blind man healed by Jesus at Bethsaida. Jesus had to lay his hands twice because, in Mark 8:24, we see that at first, the blind man said, "I see men like trees walking." Only after Jesus laid His hands on him the second time did the man fully receive his sight.

The second case to keep in mind is that of Trophimus, whom Paul had left sick in Miletus in 2 Timothy 4:20, saying, "Erastus stayed in Corinth, but Trophimus I have left in Miletus sick." It seems strange that the great apostle Paul left another servant of God, Trophimus, sick! Paul and others must have prayed and laid hands on him, but still, by the time Paul left, Trophimus was still sick, which tells us that he was not healed instantly.

The third example is found in Luke 17:11-19. Ten lepers met Jesus, standing afar off and crying out to Jesus to heal them. Jesus simply told them: "Go, show yourselves to the priests," and they were healed as they went on the way to show themselves to the priests. They were not healed instantly when Jesus spoke to them. Scripture does not tell us how far they had gone, but the point is that healing was not instant but took place a short while after.

The obstacle that faces those who are not healed instantly is the physical evidence of their sickness. They can feel or see the physical evidence of their sickness. It is this physical evidence that stands against faith. Those not healed instantly do have faith; otherwise, they would not have sought elders to lay hands on them in the first place. The problem is that the physical evidence of the lingering sickness overwhelms their faith.

Is there a way out? How can such a person be encouraged? There is surely a biblical way out! It is provided by Abraham, the father of faith. When God promised him a son, he was 100 years old, and his wife Sarah had passed the age of conceiving. How did Abraham deal with the physical evidence of his old body and the deadness of Sarah's womb? The answer is revealed in Romans 4:19, which states, "And not being weak in faith, he did not consider his own body, already dead (since he was about a hundred years old), and the deadness of Sarah's womb." The key words here are "he did not consider," implying that he accepted the fact that he was old and that Sarah had passed the age of bearing children. This was the physical evidence. How did he react to the physical evidence? He did not consider the physical evidence as an obstacle to God's promise that He would give them a child. This is the victory that overcomes physical evidence. God is not limited by physical evidence of sickness. This gives us a key when we are prayed for, and hands are laid on us, but healing is not instant; the evidence of sickness continues, the pain, the weakness, and the suffering continue! The fact is, we acknowledge the physical evidence, but we must never consider it as an obstacle to God's healing.

Armed with this understanding, we wait upon the Lord! This does not mean that we deny the physical evidence because it is surely there, but we do not consider it as something that limits God's healing power: God is never and will never be limited by physical evidence. Scripture is full of such teaching.

We also have the testimony of King David in Psalm 27:13-14. David was in a deep depression. He was going through a hard time. This was his physical evidence. He had two choices: to give in to depression and remain depressed, or to choose to believe that God was able to lift him up out of his depression and to give him better days. David chose to believe the Lord. This is what David says in Psalm 27:13, "I would have lost heart unless I had believed that I would see the goodness of the Lord in the land of the living."

Like David, when healing is not instant, we must deliberately choose to believe that we will see the goodness of the Lord right here while we live. We must choose to believe that healing is coming, though it may tarry. Once we make this choice, we follow the wisdom of Psalm 27:14, "Wait on the Lord, be of good courage, and He will strengthen your heart. Wait, I say on the Lord."

Finally, we must cultivate a renewed mindset. We must move away from the old mindset of seeing before believing to believing and then seeing. This was the issue raised by Jesus Christ to Thomas the doubter. Thomas refused to believe that Jesus had resurrected, even with evidence from the rest of the disciples. He declared he would not believe until he saw Jesus physically and touched His wounds. Well, Jesus came in at that moment and addressed Thomas by asking him to touch His wounds. Only then did Thomas believe. Jesus responded in John 20:29, "Thomas, because you have seen Me, you have believed. Blessed are those who have not seen and yet have believed."

This is the Lord's final word to those who do not receive instant healing after prayer and after hands are laid on them: blessed are you if you have believed that the healer will heal you, even though you have not yet experienced the healing!

Please remember, in His own will and wisdom, the Lord may choose to heal a person permanently by taking that person home. In that case, God will always provide the grace needed for such an outcome.

The second and third biblical purposes of laying on hands, imparting the Holy Spirit, and imparting the gifts of the Holy Spirit will be discussed in the next section.

Chapter 5

IMPARTING THE HOLY SPIRIT AND SPIRITUAL GIFTS THROUGH LAYING HANDS

"Then Peter and John laid their hands upon these believers, and they received the Holy Spirit." Acts 8:17

"For I long to see you, that I might impart to you some spiritual gift, so that you may be established, that is, that I may be encouraged together with you by the mutual faith both of you and me." Romans 1:11-12

As established in the previous sections, the Old and New Testaments attest to the laying on of hands. In the Old Testament, it was normal for a father to lay hands on family members to release a blessing, as illustrated by Jacob, when he laid hands on his son Joseph's two boys, Ephraim and Manasseh, to bless them in Genesis 48: 9-14. God specifically instructed Moses to lay his hand on Joshua in order to transfer some of his authority to him as the next leader (Numbers 27:18-23).

In the New Testament, we encounter five purposes for laying hands on people. The first purpose of transmitting divine healing (Mark 16:18) has been discussed previously. This section focuses on the second and third purposes, which are to impart the Holy Spirit and the imparting of spiritual gifts through the laying on of hands. We will look then at the biblical support in the New Testament for the laying on of hands for the purpose of imparting the Holy Spirit, as well as spiritual gifts.

The first scripture is found in Acts 8:5-17. After Philip's very successful evangelizing ministry in Samaria, following which many Samaritans believed the gospel of Jesus Christ, the new converts were baptized in water; then, when the Apostles in Jerusalem heard about

Philip's successful ministry in Samaria, they sent Peter, and John, who came and prayed for the new converts to receive the Holy Spirit baptism. The scripture explains that the converts had only been baptized in water. The ministry of laying on of hands for the purpose of baptism in the Holy Spirit is set out in Acts 8:17, which reads, "Then they laid hands on them, and they received the Holy Spirit," that is, the converts were baptized in the Holy Spirit. It must be emphasized here that the Samaritan converts had been baptized in water, and yet it was necessary for them to be baptized in the Holy Spirit for power.

The second scriptural basis for this particular ministry of imparting the Holy Spirit is in Acts 9:17. The Lord instructed Ananias to visit Saul after the Damascus experience that blinded him. Ananias laid his hands on Saul in order for him to receive the Holy Spirit and receive his sight. As soon as Saul received his sight, he was baptized in water. It is not stated specifically that Saul received the Holy Spirit when Ananias laid hands on him, but it is implied because this is the purpose for which the Lord had sent Ananias. Ananias spoke to Saul, saying, "Brother Saul, the Lord Jesus, who appeared to you on the road as you came, has sent me that you may receive your sight and be filled with the Holy Spirit."

A third scripture to support the laying on of hands to impart the Holy Spirit is in Acts 19:1-7. Paul (formerly Saul) found some disciples of John the Baptist in Ephesus. After questioning them, he found that although they had received the baptism of John, they had not been baptized with the Christian water baptism that signifies the death, burial, and resurrection of

Jesus Christ. The baptism of John did not reflect these three things because Jesus had not yet died, had not been buried, nor had he resurrected during the time of John the Baptist. His baptism was only a baptism of repentance. That was the first problem with the Ephesian disciples. Their baptism in water was that of John the Baptist and not the baptism ordained by the Lord Jesus Christ, which reflects His death, burial, and resurrection. For a detailed discussion of the difference between John the Baptist's water baptism and that ordained by Christ in the Great Commission (Matthew 28:19), refer to the author's book, BAPTISMS in the series "THE PURSUIT OF JESUS CHRIST."

The second problem with the Ephesian disciples was that they had never heard of the Holy Spirit or the baptism in the Holy Spirit. Paul had to teach them fully, and when they understood, Paul baptized them again in water with a proper Christian baptism, which is by far greater and more significant than that of John the Baptist; then what followed after water baptism is explained in Acts 19:6, "And when Paul had laid hands on them, the Holy Spirit came upon them, and they spoke in tongues, and prophesied."

Imparting spiritual gifts is the third purpose of laying on of hands, and we find this illustrated in 1 Timothy 4:14 and 2 Timothy 1:6, where we are told that church elders and Paul laid hands on Timothy to impart a spiritual gift. 1 Corinthians 12 teaches about the nine gifts of the Spirit. It should be noted here that there is a difference between the Holy Spirit and His gifts that He distributes to each believer as He chooses. As in the case of Timothy, gifts of the

Holy Spirit can be imparted by the laying on of hands.

In conclusion, we have established that laying on of hands to impart the Holy Spirit and spiritual gifts is scriptural. It is very important to understand that this ministry of laying on of hands can be done by any true believer in the Lord Jesus Christ according to His great commission in Mark 16:17-18.

It must also be remembered that the baptism in the Holy Spirit can be received without the laying on of hands. Notice, however, that one still needs to be baptized in water, even after being baptized in the Holy Spirit, in order to "fulfill all righteousness," as spoken in Matthew 3:15.

In the next section, attention will be given to the fourth and fifth purposes of laying on of hands in the New Testament: setting apart specific people for specific service unto Christ and for appointing deacons and elders in the church.

Chapter 6

SET APART FOR GOD'S SERVICE AND IN THE APPOINTMENT OF DEACONS AND ELDERS

As they ministered to the Lord and fasted, the Holy Ghost said, 'Separate me, Barnabas, and Saul for the work whereunto I have called them.' And when they had fasted, prayed, and laid their hands on them, they sent them away. So they, being sent forth by the Holy Ghost, departed unto Seleucia, and from thence they sailed to Cyprus as highlighted in Acts 13:2-4.

We have previously discussed the purposes of laying on of hands as laid out in the Old and New Testaments: for healing, for the baptism in the Holy Spirit, and for imparting spiritual gifts of the Holy Spirit. In this section, we will discuss the fourth purpose of laying on of hands: to set apart specific believers for a specific service for God, and the fifth purpose of appointment of deacons and elders of the church (Commissioning and Ordaining).

The mention of the purpose of setting apart for a specific work of God is found in Acts 13: 1-3. In the church at Antioch, the Holy Spirit said, "Now, separate to me Barnabas and Saul for the work to which I have called them." The disciples there then fasted and prayed for Barnabas and Saul, laid hands on them, and sent them away. In this case, the laying on of hands was to confirm the Holy Spirit's instructions and set apart Barnabas and Saul for the work of Christ, which was missionary in nature. By laying hands on them, the disciples at Antioch church set Barnabas and Saul apart for God's work. This ministry of setting apart for God's work is still practiced today in many churches.

Concerning laying hands on church deacons and elders, the scripture in Acts 6:1-6 confirms this particular ministry. After the congregation elected seven deacons, the Apostles then laid hands on them; the purpose was to acknowledge them, confirm their appointments publicly, and, at the same time, impart wisdom to them by laying hands on them.

It should be noted at this point that deacons were elected by the congregation to serve at tables and to serve the Apostles. Their election was then confirmed by the Apostles by the public laying on of hands. However, Elders were appointed by the Apostles themselves, and their appointments depended on the guidance of the Holy Spirit. The Apostles would spend time praying and fasting to receive guidance from the Holy Spirit for the appointment of elders. The reason for this is because the main responsibility of Elders was to give spiritual direction, as well as instructions to the congregation.

The office of an Elder is referred to by two other names: Bishop and Overseer. Although there are three titles, it is the same office and the same responsibility being referred to by three titles: it is one office only and not three. It was the accepted practice to lay hands on elders for public confirmation and imparting wisdom.

Chapter 7

RELEASING OF BLESSINGS

And he took them up in his arms, put his hands upon them, and blessed them. Mark 10:16

The act of laying hands on someone as a way to release blessings holds a powerful spiritual meaning. When done in faith, it becomes a channel through which God's grace can flow. Whether it's passing on a blessing like Jacob did or showing divine favor as Jesus did with the children, this practice reflects the belief that God uses people to carry out His plans.

In both Genesis 48:14 and Mark 10:16, the act of laying on hands is not passive. It is a deliberate, intentional action that speaks of God's desire to bless, empower, and uplift His people. For those in ministry or anyone who prays for others, it serves as a powerful reminder that we are conduits of God's goodness, entrusted with the privilege of releasing His blessings into the lives of those around us.

When we lay hands on someone to bless them, we stand in the gap between heaven and earth, facilitating a divine exchange. We become participants in fulfilling God's promises, just as Jacob and Jesus did. Through this sacred act, God's blessings—whether they be spiritual, emotional, or physical—are released, changing lives and fulfilling His purposes.

In Genesis 48, Jacob (Israel) lays his hands on his grandsons Ephraim and Manasseh to bestow a blessing. What stands out in this account is the intentionality with which Jacob places his right hand on Ephraim, the younger son, and his left hand on Manasseh, the elder. Traditionally, the right hand was reserved for the firstborn, symbolizing greater blessing and inheritance. However, Jacob crosses his hands, signifying God's sovereign choice to bless Ephraim with a greater portion, even though he was the younger.

Laying on hands was not merely a familial tradition but a prophetic declaration of God's plans for the two boys. By laying his hands on them, Jacob was aligning himself with the will of God, transferring not just material inheritance but also divine favor. It teaches us that when hands are laid upon someone in the context of prayer or blessing, it is not a human action alone—it is a partnership with God in releasing His predetermined purposes. Jacob's blessing was more than words. His hands, directed by God's wisdom, became instruments of destiny.

In Mark 10:16, Jesus welcomes little children and lays His hands on them to bless them.

The disciples initially tried to prevent the children from approaching Him, viewing them as a distraction. But Jesus rebukes the disciples in Mark 10:14, saying, "Let the little children come to me, and do not hinder them, for the kingdom of God belongs to such as these." He then takes the children in His arms, lays His hands on them, and blesses them.

This simple yet profound moment captures the heart of Jesus toward humanity. By laying His hands on the children, Jesus did more than show affection; He was imparting divine blessing and affirming their value in the Kingdom of God. The laying on of hands here signifies acceptance, protection, and favor. It speaks to the powerful truth that everyone, regardless of age or status, is worthy of God's blessing.

Furthermore, the children's example of openness and humility is a picture of how we must approach the Lord to receive His blessings. The act of laying hands on them was a physical manifestation of the spiritual reality that God's grace is freely given to those who come to Him in faith. This passage teaches us that through the laying on of hands, we not only receive blessings but also are brought into a closer relationship with God, experiencing His love in a tangible way.

Whether we are laying hands on others to bless, heal, or commission them, we are participating in God's greater purpose for their lives, releasing His power and favor into the world.

Chapter 8

DANGERS OF LAYING ON OF HANDS

"Do not lay hands on anyone hastily, nor share in other people's sins; keep yourself pure." I Timothy 5:22

We have established that the ministry of laying on of hands is backed by scripture and is of great significance in the life of a believer. Our Lord and Savior, Jesus Christ, practiced it and instructed that it should accompany the preaching of the gospel. Believers are expected to lay hands on the sick for the purpose of healing, as well as other purposes, as listed above. However, as important as the ministry of laying on hands is, there are certain dangers that all should be aware of. When we examine scripture, we discover those dangers are in laying hands hastily, laying hands if you are spiritually contaminated, laying hands for manipulation or control, laying hands and imparting the wrong spirit, or laying hands without faith or spiritual preparedness. This section will investigate the nature of these dangers and how to avoid them.

In 1 Timothy 5:22, Paul warned young Timothy not to lay hands on anybody hastily and explained why, advising, "Do not share in other people's sins." In other words, do not make yourself accountable for their sins or share in their sins by laying hands on them. Paul warned Timothy not to rush to ordain ministers before proving them to be fit for the office they were appointed to because any mistakes or sins committed by those hastily ordained would be blamed on him. The person to be ordained should be one already producing the fruit of righteousness and not one living in sin. If Timothy ordained individuals who were living a secret life of sin, it would imply that

Timothy was condoning such sinful habits and, therefore, agreeing with them. In this manner, he would be partaking of their sins, not only in ordaining them but also in laying hands on them. Paul then advised Timothy and all believers how to avoid this mistake: by keeping oneself pure, in this case, by adhering to strict discipline and not condoning sin.

However, there is another aspect of laying on of hands in which the warning "not to share in other people's sin" is particularly important. If the spirit of a person who is laid hands on is not clean due to unconfessed sin, the spirit of the person laying hands on that person can be affected negatively. It can also happen the other way around. If the person laying hands has hidden and unconfessed sin, like sexual immorality, that spirit of immorality will be transferred onto the person who is being laid hands on. The person may develop an intense desire to commit sexual immorality without understanding where such a desire came from because he did not have it before. This is an example of sharing in other people's sins. In other words, negative or unclean spirits are transferrable either way in the process of laying on hands. There can be a cross-transfer of other sins, such as lying, a critical spirit, false beliefs, depression, etc.

It must also be remembered that Satan has his servants masquerading as ministers of light, and in the case of laying hands on people to receive the baptism in the Holy Spirit, these servants of Satan will lay hands on people to transfer a satanic imitation of the Holy Spirit. The person who receives such a satanic spirit will soon discover that everything begins to go wrong in his life. Examples of negative results would include a sudden loss of interest in reading the bible, praying, going to church, and disinterest in hearing the word of God or even hearing people talk about the Lord Jesus Christ. False tongues can originate from Satan. Such a person negatively impacted in this manner will eventually need deliverance to be set free.

Some time ago, I met a lady who ministers with her husband in a church where the husband is the Senior Pastor. Both of them officiate marriages. The lady told me that she has officiated 21 marriages, while her husband has done 37 marriages. She had observed that of all the couples she has joined in marriage, only one couple has divorced, while nearly 80 percent of the couples joined by her husband have divorced. She, therefore, sought the Lord in prayer to find out why. The Lord revealed to her that her husband came from a very dysfunctional family, and the same spirit has been transferred to the couples he has joined. All the couples were laid hands on during the marriage ceremony. The lady herself comes from a good family with no marital issues. This is a good illustration of the danger that exists in the ministry of laying on of hands.

In Leviticus 16:21, Aaron was instructed by God through Moses to lay his hands on the head of the scapegoat while confessing the sins of Israel, and in this manner, he would be putting them on the head of the goat. This is biblical evidence that something spiritual is transferred whenever hands are laid on a person. That which is transferred can be either positive, negative, or both.

Scripture, however, offers ways to guard ourselves against these. First, the ministry of laying on of hands must be preceded by prayer.

Secondly, we must be guided by the Holy Spirit in everything we do pertaining to the laying on of hands. Thirdly, we must cover ourselves with the blood of Jesus Christ. Fourthly, we must be empowered or anointed by the Holy Spirit to stand against any demonic influence from the person we are laying hands on. Fifthly, we must live righteously and produce the fruit of righteousness.

Our Lord Jesus Christ gives one important key in Matthew 7:16, as He warned about false prophets, saying, "You will know them by their fruits." This is an obvious reason why Paul warned Timothy not to lay hands on any man hastily before seeing their fruits of right living. Sometimes, believers may attend a crusade or are invited by a friend to go and listen to a special guest speaker. Special speakers are also invited to speak by particular churches. These guest speakers may invite people to be prayed for, and in the process of praying, the guest speaker may lay hands on those being prayed for. In such a situation, believers may not know what kind of life the speaker lives or whether the guest speaker manifests fruits of righteousness or not. In a situation like this, the scriptural safeguards mentioned above become very handy, and the person who may desire to be laid hands on by a guest speaker whose fruit is not known is well warned to apply these safeguards before hands are laid on that person by a guest speaker.

The warning about laying on of hands is similar to the danger that exists in a church where the minister in that church has hidden unconfessed sins like immorality. The spirit of immorality operating in the minister will be passed on to the congregation members, who may, in time, begin to engage in the same sin operating in the life of the church minister. The opposite is also true: a spirit of righteousness in a minister's life will impact the congregation's lives.

CONCLUDING REMARKS

In concluding the discussion of the ministry of laying on of hands, we see that this ministry is very important. It is backed by scripture and approved by the Lord and should not be taken lightly. It must, however, be remembered that care should be taken to avoid cross-contamination or the partaking of unclean spirits. Guidance from the Holy Spirit is essential to the person laying hands. The person must be living right and must ask the Lord for the cover of his precious blood before the ministry.

Finally, all should be aware that salvation comes through the laying on of hands by faith in Jesus Christ, through which the supernatural power of God transfers our sins onto Christ at the cross. He who knew no sin became sin for us: 2 Corinthians 5:21. This transfer is reflected in the scapegoat principle in Leviticus 16: 21-22. During the feast of atonement, which was once a year, Aaron, the High Priest during the time of Moses, was instructed to lay his hands on the head of the scapegoat and to confess the sins of Israel over the head of the goat. By doing so, God said that Aaron would be putting the sins of the people onto the head of the goat. The goat was then led out by a chosen person to the wilderness as the congregation watched the goat carrying their sins away. This is a very powerful illustration that, indeed, something spiritual is transferred when hands are laid on a person: as Aaron laid his hands on the goat, the sins of the people were transferred to the goat, and to prove it, God was satisfied with this process for one year. That's right, the people remained forgiven for one year!

When Jesus Christ carried the sin of the world to the cross, a wonderful provision was provided by God. Every person who believes in this provision of grace is forgiven not for one year but permanently. This is the reason why Romans 8:1 declares, "There is, therefore, no condemnation to those who are in Christ Jesus, who do not walk according to the flesh, but according to the Spirit." Remember, however, that everyone who is forgiven in this manner has the responsibility to walk after the Spirit and not after the flesh. Walking after the flesh means obeying the desires of our flesh, but as Paul the Apostle points out in Romans 7:18, "For I know that in me (that is, in my flesh) nothing good dwells." Sin, Paul says, dwells in the flesh; the desires of the flesh are consequently sinful. The flesh produces the works of the flesh listed in Galatians 5:19-21 that are contrary to the will of God.

Walking after the Spirit is the very opposite of walking after the flesh. Walking after the Spirit of God involves obeying the guidance of the Holy Spirit in everything that a believer does. The outcome of walking after the spirit is the fruit of the Spirit as listed in Galatians 5:22-23. For one who walks after the Spirit of God, there is no condemnation now in this life and in the life to come, when all believers stand before the Judgment Seat of Christ for rewards according to one's works while living.

About The Author

The Reverend Chaplain Edward Karanja was born and raised in Gikuni Village, Kiambu district in Kenya. He is the last of eight children born to the late Reverend Ruben Karanja and his late spouse, Rebecca. Edward was born again in 1971, during a bible study group while attending Nairobi University. He later graduated with a Bachelor of Commerce in Business Administration. From that time forward, Edward felt the call of God in his life and began to experience a strong desire to teach and explain scripture in a simple yet in-depth way.

After realizing he still needed more experience and God's anointing, Edward became ordained as a Lay Leader in 1987 at the Mombasa Cathedral Anglican Church, where he ministered part-time for several years. During this time and in this church, Edward began to teach bible study, which continued for 15 years. At the same time, Edward was employed by SGS Kenya Limited, where he served as the branch manager in Mombasa for 25 years. He was later promoted and transferred to Kampala, Uganda, as SGS Uganda's country managing director. While in Uganda, Edward continued teaching bible study at Upper Room Ministries, catering to college students.

In 2001, Edward and his family immigrated to the United States, where he continued his education at Beulah Heights University in Atlanta, GA. In 2003, Edward graduated with Honors (Summa Cum Laude) with his second bachelor's degree, this time in Biblical Education. He was awarded the University's All-American Scholar Award, nominated to the National Dean's List, and Who's Who Among Students in American Universities and Colleges in recognition of outstanding merit and accomplishment as a student at Beulah University, 2003-2004. Edward also received Scholastic Membership from the National Honor Society of The Accrediting Association of Bible Colleges (DELTA EPISILION CHI). In 2004, Edward was awarded a Standard Teacher's

Diploma by the Evangelical Training Association through Beulah Heights University, granting him permanent approval to teach certificate courses.

In 2024, Edward earned a doctorate in Biblical Exposition at Andersonville Theological Seminary, Camilla, Georgia, USA.

In 2007, Edward completed his Clinical Pastoral Education, ACPE, and CPE Chaplains Residency program at St Joseph's Hospital in Atlanta, GA, and continues serving as a chaplain for Vitas Healthcare Services. In 2004, Edward also became ordained at Elim Victory Church International in Marietta, GA, where he has been ministering and continues to teach bible study. Edward is married to Pastor Tabitha, his spouse of 48 years. They have a daughter, two sons, and four grandchildren. Edward and Tabitha are also the founders of the Destiny of Christians International Ministries.

Edward is the author of two other books, Repentance and Faith and Baptisms, in the series "The Pursuit of Christ."

DESTINY OF CHRISTIANS INTERNATIONAL MINISTRY
DOC
Destiny of Christians
INTERNATIONAL MINISTRIES
Rev Chaplain Edward Karanja
and Pastor Tabitha Karanja
• Reeling from the death of a loved one?
• Overwhelmed, stressed & anxious?
• Wondering what is next on your Christian journey?
You are not alone! We are here to help.
At DOC Ministries we offer:
BEREAVEMENT COUNSELING
BIBLICAL COUNSELING
FAMILY COUNSELING
/docintlministries
Destiny of Christians International Ministries
docministries2019@gmail.com
www.destinyofchristians.org
LIVE
Every Wednesday at 8:00 PM

Made in the USA
Columbia, SC
13 April 2025